RAISING GOATS

FOR BEGINNERS

Table of contents

INTRODUCTION

Thank you for choosing Raising Goats for Beginners: The Ultimate Guide to Raising a Happy and Healthy herd of Goats – Breed Selection, Sheltering, feeding, Goat Care Breeding, Milking and More.

Goats are a versatile animal to be raised in your backyard. They are straightforward to deal with, they are a source of low-fat meat, and they also produce milk in a large quantity. Goat's manure makes a great source of fertilizer to your farm's crop too. Adequate land is required for goats foraging or grazing and well-built fencing. Apart from that, raising goats is as easy as any other farm animals.

Male baby goats are referred to as BUCKLINGS or BUCKS. Female baby goats are referred to as

DOELINGS or DOES. A castrated (neutered with simple rubber banding) male goat is called WETHER.

Getting a female goat pregnant in order for her to have babies first is the only way to get milk from goats. Whenever a goat delivers babies, it initiates her production of milk, and this is called FRESHENING. Just like humans, the mother has a lot of milk at first, but the amount of milk gradually decreases over roughly one year.

Usually, goats deliver their babies during the spring; then, you can sell the babies when they reach eight weeks old and enjoy the milk for about the whole year. You will need to breed your goat again during the fall if you desire to freshen her milk once more during the spring. Do not bother; you can still mil your doe during pregnancy, but you need to give her two months to dry up before the delivery time, for her to boost some nutritional reserves for her babies.

CHAPTER 1: BENEFITS OF RAISING GOATS

For homesteaders, hobby farmers, and small farmers alike, goats can be a great choice of animals. They are lovely when it comes to meat, milk, fiber, and more. Here are some of the benefits of raising goats:

Raise Your Own Meat

Keeping goats for meat is an excellent thing to do for you and your family to take care of your food needs. It can also serve as a lucrative small farm business – if well maintained and you know where you can quickly sell your goats.

Milk Production

Dairy goats produce plentiful amounts of milk, typically beyond what can be used by a family. You can make goat yogurt, goat cheese, and any other dairy products you can think of. Goats will help you accomplish a goal of producing value-added products such as yogurt and cheese if you are a small farmer. You can also sell fresh goat milk. A good market is available for it with people who don't like cow milk.

Soap Production

People with sensitive skin make use of soft and mild soap, and this kind of wonderful soap can be made with goat milk.

Fiber Production

Goats are so versatile that they can be used for meat as well as milk and fiber. Pygora and angora goats yield mohair, whereas cashmere goats produce cashmere. Also, raw goat fiber can be turned into a weave, yarn and knit, or crocheted into several valuable products.

Use Goat to Clear Land

Goats are fantastic when it comes to browsing, plus they like eating blackberry bramble and weeds. Place your goats outside to pasture on anything you want to clear-out and allow them to act as living hogs.

Goats can be Used as Pack Animals

You can train goats to carry your gear on hikes, and they are particularly apt at steep and rocky pathways. They can conveniently carry twenty to thirty percent of their body weight and their ecological impact is minimal. You do not have to pack food for your goats as they could consume whatever they find eatable by browsing along the path as they travel. You can also train your goats to pull carts.

Use their Hide and Skin

Goat hides (without hair removed) are traditionally used in Africa to make drum heads. You can dry and tan goat skins like leather, and this can be used for many value-added products such as goatskin gloves. You can also make a goatskin rug.

They eat food scraps

Aside from the fact that goats are excellent browsers, they can clear out all your leftover food, and this act is appreciably reducing the garbage in your yard.

Goats Make Manure

Their manure is beneficial for fertilizing your field. The manure an average goat produces yearly is more than a ton, and their feces come in the form of a pellet, which makes them be easily handled. Goat manure is rich in nitrogen, potash, potassium, and probably other minerals as well.

They are Easy to Handle and Train

Goats are social animals that make them very easy to handle and trouble-free to train, even by children. Also, goats are a good size when compared to cows, sheep, horses, and other larger domestic animals; so, their small size makes handling them easier.

Goats are Economical to Keep

They aren't only useful, but they are also thrifty. Owing to the fact that goats can browse and do not need an excessively fancy shelter, they can be a very cheap to run animal, especially for the small farm owner.

CHAPTER 2: GETTING STARTED

Here is some basic info to help you get started with raising goats:

Define Your Goals for Raising Goats

Prior to buying any goats, it is important that you reflect on why you want them. Do you want to keep them for milk or meat? Or do you just want to raise them as pets? Your answers to these questions will determine what breed of goat to purchase and how you will raise them. Raising goats is a considerable commitment – you will need to feed them every day, be responsible for their veterinary and food bills, and make sure they're happy and healthy – so you must be well-prepared for this responsibility.

Select a Breed that Suits Your Needs

As mentioned above, your aim for keeping goats will determine the type of goat you will choose, whether you want them for meat, milk, or as pets. You'll also need to consider the care requirements, temperament, and size of breeds. The following are some of the most famous goat's breeds:

Dairy Breeds: Oberhasli, Alpine, La Mancha, Toggenburg, Saanen, Nigerian Dwarf, Sable, and. Nubian.

Meat Breeds: Boer, Genemaster, Kiko, Tennessee, Moneymaker, Savannah, Spanish, and Texmaster.

Fiber Breeds: Angora (which produces Mohair), Cashmere, Pygora, and Nigora.

Pet Breeds: Miniature goat such as Pygmy Goats, Nigerian Dwarfs, and Kinder are great as pets.

Think About Your Available Space

Idyllically, there should be a large outdoor space where your goats would be able to browse, range, and get the needed exercise for them to stay healthy. Also, the goats will need an indoor space for shelter and rest. Generally, for every adult goat of standard size, you should provide ten to fifteen feet of space. Slightly less space will do for miniature breeds. It is imperative not to keep your goats in confined spaces or overcrowd them. Doing this will make them to become stressed and unhealthy and can promote the spread of disease.

Choose Healthy Goats

When buying your herd of goats, select the goats that are in the best physical condition. It is essential to opt for the healthiest-looking goats to avoid buying an unhealthy or sick that doesn't match your needs.

Look for alert goats with bright eyes and that walk around easily and quickly with an even step. Check if there are any bumps or lumps on the goat's body by running your hands over their body – this will show the presence of an abscess. Inspect the droppings of the goats to ensure they're solid and not runny.

Opt for goat with wide-set hips, deep-rounded bellies, and big milk sacks with descending-pointing udders (in does). Also, you should attempt milking any does you intend to buy if possible, to ascertain they are in good state and that the milk flows smoothly.

If you are buying dairy goats, ensure they're friendly and not skittish because you will want to get close to them to milk them.

Select Does Over Bucks and Wethers

You are advised to buy only female goats for a start (does) since only they can produce milk and bear kids. Male goats (buck) can begin to smell and become aggressive as they grow older. The pheromones released by bucks may also affect the taste of the milk produce by does if they're kept close to each other. Except if you wish to raise a large herd of goats, it is advisable to borrow a buck when you need one for breeding, instead of buying one yourself. The castrated male goats are wethers, and you only keep them to provide meat or as pets.

Take the Age of the Does into Consideration

When it comes to purchasing does, you have several options. The option you choose will depend on the amount you intend to spend and how soon you want your goats to have kids or produce milk. Here are the options:

I. **Purchase a baby doe**: A baby doe or doeling must be up to eight weeks old before it can be weaned from its mother. Baby does are somewhat inexpensive to buy, but it will take approximately a year and a half before they can be bred and additional five months before producing milk.

II. **Purchase a junior doe**: A junior doe is a young female goat that is yet to be bred. Junior does are more costly when compared with baby-does since you do not have to stay for that long to breed them and begin to produce milk. You can also purchase a young doe that has already been bred (for example pregnant doe), so you will only have five months to wait for her to start to produce milk. In this kind of scenario, you will need to pay a breeding fee.

III. **Purchase a doe in milk**: The last option is to purchase a mature doe that has already producing milk. This final option is cheaper and faster than the previous ones. Nevertheless, the risk that the female goat you purchase will have problems is higher because breeders would usually prefer to dispose of the feeblest animals in their yard.

Start with At Least Two Goats

Bear in mind that goats are herd animals; this implies that they love to live as a group. So, you will need to buy at least two goats for a start. A lot of people make the mistake of purchasing only one goat. A single goat will get lonely and becomes very loud as it bleats and calls out for companionship.

If possible, it's better to purchase two goats from one herd – particularly if they are related. It will assist them in adjusting to the new environment much more rapidly. Goats will, under normal circumstances, bond with other hoofed animals, such as horses, cows, sheep, so if you have already owned some of these animals, this is an option.

CHAPTER 3: HOUSING AND FEEDING YOUR GOATS

Shelter Your Goats Properly

As mentioned previously, goats will need a covered indoor area for feeding, sleeping, and defense against the night-time predator and weather. The housing doesn't have to be very elaborate, as long as there is ample outdoor space for the goats to roam around during the day time. The housing does not have to be too large as goats love to sleep together in small clusters.

The only thing you need to do is to ensure that the shelter is always dehydrated and free of draft. It is also important that you prepare a miniature stall where injured, sick, and heavily pregnant goats can be placed. You must cover the floor of the shelter in a thick layer of beddings, consisting of waste hays (anything excluding cedar), straw, or wood shavings.

Build a Goat-Proof Fence

Goats are notorious escapers as they can jump over fences, climb trees, and writhe their way through small spaces. For that reason, it is crucial that you build a sturdy, goat-proof fence around the enclosed area. Build a fence of at least 4 feet high, or 5 feet for more active goat breeds like Nubians. Chain-link, stock panel, or wooden fences are all excellent options if you're constructing a new fence. Nevertheless, you can make use of smooth electrified wire with high tensile if you only want to goat-proof and existing fence. Also, ensure that you brace any fence posts or gates on the outer surface of the fence in order to prevent goats from climbing them. Also, ensure that the shelter for the goat s doesn't have a roof that can be easily climbed.

Give Room for Your Goats to Browse

Goats love browsing rather than grazing, which implies that they prefer eating weeds, leaves, and twigs rather than plain grass. This characteristic makes it possible to raise goats alongside horses, cows, and sheep because they don't compete for food. You can also use goats to clear rough piece of land and eliminate unwanted plants. If you reside in a wooded or green, rural setting, don't hesitate to put your goats outside to pasture and allow them to forage for stuff like poison ivy and clover, blackberry canes, shrubs, sapling, etc.

Provide Hay and Grain for Your Goats

Goats cannot acquire all their needed nourishment from browsing alone, so you will want to supply them with enough top-quality hay or other forage crops. You can provide them with hay free-choice; therefore, they can eat as much or as little they like.

Pregnant goats or those producing milk will require additional protein, so they will also need a few pounds of grain daily. Also, you should provide a good free-choice mineral block or mineral mix for your goats. You will get this in most feed stores. When it comes to treats, you can supply your goats with varieties of vegetables and fruit such as carrots, spinach, squash, celery, banana, apples, watermelon, peaches, and pears. Just avoid feeding them kale, tomatoes, and potatoes as they can be poisonous to goats.

Give Your Goats Plenty of Water

Your goats must always have access to clean water, especially during dry and hot weather. Therefore, depending on the weather conditions, you will want to give your goats ½ gallon (1.9 liters) to 4gallons (15.1 liters) of water daily.

It is important to sketch out in advance how you intend to supply water to your goats because you will not want to keep moving buckets of water now and then to their shelter on a daily basis. If you do not have one already, think about installing a stock tank or digging a water line to your goats' shelter.

If you have a pond or creek on your property, this is an easy way to make sure that your goats are always hydrated. Nevertheless, ensure you test the water first to ascertain that it's drinkable. Also, you will need to watch out for stagnation or contamination.

CHAPTER 4: BREEDING AND MILKING YOUR GOATS

Breed Your Goats When the Does is Mature

Goats are to be bred when the does have reached maturity. The maturity stage for standard goats is six months old, or when they weigh no less than sixty pounds, they're ready for breeding. Their annual heat cycles usually start around August or September. Feel-free to hire a buck or take your doe/does to a farm that has a buck if you do not have one. You will be asked to make a stud payment of around fifty to one-hundred dollars ($50 to $100).

It is difficult to know if a doe is pregnant, so the milky-white discharge coming from her nether region is one of the best signs of successful mating. The pregnancy of a goat lasts for five months or 150 days and most of the pregnancies tend to deliver 2 babies, and in some cases it may be up to 4.

Determine How You Desire To Raise Your Kid Goats

As soon as the kid goats has been delivered, make sure you thoroughly clean them with a cloth to get rid of any birthing substance or blood, or better still, let the mother do the cleaning by licking them. Start from this stage, when we talk about caring for and feeding the kids, there are 2 schools of thought.

A school of thought prefers to separate the baby goats from the mother instantly. They usually milk the mother by hands and then pour the milk inside the bottle to feed the baby goats. They do this because it is believed that it can be difficult to wean baby goats and this will result in the mother goat producing less milk. It is also in their opinion that bottle-fed goats will be friendlier and tamer.

Nevertheless, the second school of thought is of the opinion that separating baby goats from their mother is unnecessary and cruel. They permit the kids to be fed by their mother directly (though you will need to give them proper attention to ensure all of the kids are well fed), and when they are between 8 and 12 weeks old (ready to be weaned), they will now separate the kids from their mother. Which style you decide to adopt out of the two is a matter of choice and whether you value a more natural process or increased milk production.

Define What to Do With the Baby Goats

If increasing the size of your herd is not in your line of interest, you will want to settle on what to do with the kids. It is usually easy to deal with young does since there is a high demand for milk-producing does. So, young does can be sold to other goat owners immediately after they are weaned. If desired, you may retain the female kid of your best milk producer so that she will take the position of her mother in the future.

It is somewhat challenging to deal with bucks. Most immature bucks ought to be castrated as soon as they are about 3 to 4 weeks old since you will eventually sell them for meat. This can be done shortly after they are weaned or delayed until they reach maturity. One buck can be kept as a breeding sire.

Get To Know the Lactation Cycle

A doe will begin to produce milk immediately after she has delivered her first kids, and she will continue producing milk for about 305 days (ten months) after delivery. The flow of milk is normally at the peak two to three months after delivery, diminishing towards the end of the lactation cycle. A two-month "dry spell" will be required for the doe before giving birth a second time - in the dairy world, this period is called "freshening."

If you are a novice in milking an animal, it's imperative to get the procedure right, so you don't tug on the teat. What you need to do is to wrap your hand around the teat, cut off the milk supply at the top with your forefinger and thumb and then squeeze the teat and extract the milk with the other fingers.

You may find milking to be slightly slow and inconvenient at the start, and it can take you about thirty minutes on one goat. But once you become familiar with it, you will able to do it within a short period.

It is recommended that you do milking once in the morning and once at night. Standard-sized goats will produce approximately 3 quarts of milk daily during peak production, while what miniature goats like the

Nigerian dwarf will produce is a bit less.

CHAPTER 5: KEEPING YOUR GOATS SAFE AND HEALTHY

Protect Your Goats from Predators

It is essential to know about the predators in your neighborhood, so you will be able to take actions towards protecting your goats.

Cougars, coyotes, dogs, and birds such as vultures and ravens are common goat predators. Some of these predators are capable of carrying your goats (especially the baby goats) away, while others will inflict injury on them to the extent that you will need to put them down.

The most suitable way of ensuring the safety of your goats is by locking them in a protected building (without open doors or windows) every night. Also, you should think about getting a livestock guardian dog to keep away predators all the time.

The United States Department of Agriculture (USDA) recommends that you can hang the carcass of a vulture (which does not have to be real) from a post or tree in order to discourage vultures. Also, try to shun the habit of tethering your goats because it will make them an easy target for any predator. It is much safer to leave them in an enclosed space that has a high fence.

Learn To Identify the Signs and Symptoms of a Sick Goat

You will unavoidably have to encounter a sick goat once in a while so it is essential that you can interpret the signs. The familiar and noticeable signs and symptoms of a sick goat include: inability to eat, inability to drink, hot udders, diarrhea, crusty eyes, grinding teeth, pale eyelids, and grey gums, coughing, crying or calling more than usual, pressing its face against fence or wall, isolating itself.

You are advised to call the veterinarian to attend to your goat as soon as you notice any of these symptoms so it can stand a higher chance of becoming fully healthy again. Yearly vaccinations against enterotoxaemia and tetanus will also be needed by your goats. It is also vital that you be wary of parasites like ticks and lice.

Ensure to Always Clean and Trim Your Goats

Generally, goats do not demand excessive grooming (except the varieties with long hair), but you will want to attend to them from time to time to make sure they are clean and comfortable. Here is what you need to do to ensure your goats are cleaned:

I. **Brushing and Bating of Goats**: Goats must be brushed once a year as a minimum (preferably at the beginning of summer when they are shedding) with a hard-bristled grooming brush. This will remove loose hair and dandruff, stimulate the flow of blood, and allow you to inspect for any lumps on the skin or other signs and symptoms of ailments. Bathing your goat isn't a must, but it assists in removing lice and make clipping more straightforward.

II. **Clipping Your Goats Hair**: Clipping of your goats' hair is required at least yearly in order to help them stay cool all through the summer. Clipping the tail and udder areas of female goats more often may be necessary to help them stay clean during kidding and milking season. If you intend to enter your goats in shows, you will want to clip and bathe them more often.

III. **Trimming Goats' Hooves**: You are required to trim the hooves of your goats at least once in a month; if not, they will overgrow and hard to walk on. Trimming is a relatively easy and quick process, which can be done with a roofing or packet knife.

CHAPTER 6: CARING FOR A PREGNANT DOE

The pregnancy of a goat lasts 150 days or five months. A pregnant doe can be milked until two months prior to delivery. At this time, they naturally begin drying up, but you will want to encourage this to occur. All it required to help dry up a goat is for you to reduce milking. You can reduce milking to every other day, then every few days. By this time, you will stop drinking the milk because it will taste salty as the mineral build-up is too high.

Ensure that you de-worm and supplement their diet in the last two months with some leftover scraps from your kitchen. At this time, vegetables and fruit can be little nutritional boost fun treats for them. A small organic grain will also serve as a treat, but not too much of it. Usually, animals consumed a leftover grain from the fall harvest, but the grain can be acidic to a goat's body as it's hard to digest. A number of people are of the opinion that animals with rumen stomachs should not consume grain at all, but I believe a little once in a while is just ok. I usually soak the grain or sprout prior to giving it in order to help digestibility.

Run your fingers alongside your goat's spine to the tail to know that she is getting close to delivery. While running your hand, just before you reach her tail, see if you can squeeze the ligament. You will observe a specific relaxing of that ligament if you do this around two to three weeks prior to delivery. Once you notice it is totally gone, you should be expecting her to deliver within a couple of days.

CHAPTER 7: HOW MUCH MILK DOES A GOAT PRODUCE?

When I was searching for a better dairy breed, the flavor and taste of their milk is all I cared for. I tried the milk of a couple of different breeds, and I found some with this typical musky flavor. But when I tried the milk of the Nigeria Dwarf Goat, I was amazed! It is extremely smooth, fresh, and somewhat sweet with no any kind of aftertaste. I got to know that the Nigerian Dwarfs were purposely bred to produce milk that tastes like cow's milk. Therefore, I'm recommending the Nigerian Dwarfs for the best flavoring milk. The Nigerian Dwarf Goats are smaller in size than other breeds, consuming less hay, which is a plus. A full-grown Nigeria Dwarf is approximately 75 lbs.

This info is for a Nigerian Dwarf Goat (my favorite). They are called Dwarfs due to their small size. Undoubtedly, large goats produce more milk.

Once a Nigeria Dwarf goat freshens or delivers babies, her udder will start to operate at full capacity. When the kids have reached two weeks, you can begin to milk your goat. The mother should be separated from the babies at night to allow her udder to fill up overnight. She will have a large udder filled with milk in the morning, and you can milk out enough before releasing her for her offspring for the rest of the day.

You don't have to worry about the milk for the babies. The amazing thing about goats is that they have a reflex that naturally holds back milk for their kids. Therefore, when you're milking in the morning, you will be able to milk until the milk stops coming out. You will understand she wants you to stop by this time because when you continue squeezing, nothing will come out of her udder.

Once it reaches eight weeks old, when you can wean the babies, you can then be milking your goats morning and night. By this time, your doe will be at the peak of her production. During this period, my Nigerian Dwarf goat produces approximately a quart or more in the morning and the same amount at night. So, in a day, she produces ½ gallons or 15 gallons per month.

Your goat's milk production will begin to drop gradually. When it gets to about five to six months after freshening, a Nigerian Dwarf goat will produce approximately three cups of milk in the morning and the same amount at night. So, in a day, she produces 1½ quarts or 11 gallons per month. Your doe will be at two cups in the morning and about the same amount at night when it gets to about eight to nine months after freshening. Total milk production in a day is about one quart or 7 gallons per month.

Once your goat is pregnant, her milk will keep drying up, and you ought to stop milking when it reaches ten months. If your goat isn't pregnant, she might keep producing milk for up to two years, depending on the individual goat.

CHAPTER 8: KEEPING RAW GOAT'S MILK FRESH AND DELICIOUS

Debunk the myth that goat's milk tastes pungent and has a musky flavor. If you have not had fresh raw goat's milk, trust me, you're missing out because goat's milk is light, clean, sweet, and fresh tasting. However, there are some things that can change the goat's milk taste. For example, goats are sensitive to pheromones so, if you keep a buck (male) in close quarters with a doe (female), the chance that the milk will taste musky is very high. The pheromone male goats give off is very strong such that it can affect the does hormones and her milk's flavor. To avoid this problem, keep your buck (if you plan to have one) far away from does except during breeding.

Another thing that can alter the taste of goat's milk is how it's being handled after milking. The following tips will help you in keeping your raw goat's milk fresh and tasty for two weeks or more:

Begin the Milking With a Clean Stainless Steel Bucket

Milk will turn hard and be attached to your milk bucket over time, so using a seamless stainless bucket is a great option when it comes to keeping your goat's milk as clean and as fresh as possible. Rinse out the bucket with cool water after milking; next, spray it with a natural cleanser, and then rinse again with hot water. You need to start with cool water because hot water will harden the milk and bring about milk stone if you use it in milk, and this will lead to a build-up of old milk that can alter the taste of your milk faster. Therefore, bear in mind to use cool water to rinse the milking bucket first, then wash with soap and rinse again with hot water. If you are dealing with the Nigerian dwarf goat, try to get to a short stainless bucket to fit under it when milking.

Filter Your Milk Immediately

If you have ever milked an animal before, you know that flecks, bugs, hair, and dirt of whatsoever can get into your milk. It is essential to strain every little spot out of your milk to keep it fresh and delicious. I usually make use of special disposable milk filters and hold the filter with a stainless steel strainer.

Refrigerate Your Milk Immediately

Place your milk in the fridge shortly after filtering and keep it between 35° and 38°. For you to make raw milk maintain its fresh taste for a long time make sure you do not break the "cold chain" (Mark McAfee of Organic Pastures Dairy). I used to keep my raw goat's milk in my regular refrigerator and noticed it did not last long before it tasted off. I realized that my regular refrigerator, even at its coolest, is around forty degrees –hence the reason why my goat's milk only lasted about five days before losing taste. I decided to buy a mini-refrigerator, and that was the best thing I could have done to preserve my raw goat's milk as it worked wonderfully. A normal small refrigerator will contain four gallons of milk, which is more than enough for the goats' keepers.

Store Your Milk in a Glass Jar

The most suitable place to store raw milk is glass. I prefer using mason jars and plastic lids, but there are other glass jar options. To clean and sterilize your jars, rinse them with cold water, use a natural cleaner and hot water to spray, and then run them through the dishwasher. One or two times a month, you can make use of 2 tablespoons of 3 percent Hydrogen Peroxide and shake within the jar and let soak prior to placing in the dishwasher.

CHAPTER 9: HOW TO USE YOUR GOAT'S MILK

There are numerous things you can use your goat's milk for. If you are familiar with goat's milk, you may put it to use without delay; if you aren't, it might rather be intimidating. If all you have ever known has been cow's milk, you might be skeptical about it. The moment you dip your toes into homesteading and begin to raise your own goats, you will know how pleasant and amazing it is for its uses. Here are some of the things you can do with your goat's milk:

Drink It Up

You can do a lot of things with your goat's milk, and one of them is to drink it. To some people, drinking goat's milk may seem odd, or maybe not. But the fact is, goat's milk isn't only nutritious, but it's also far better for you than cow's milk.

Pour It Out

Pour your goat's milk over cereal, which means you can use goat's milk to substitute cow's milk. It is perfect with granola or cereal. When you are out of your regular store-bought milk, rather than running to the grocery store, make do with your goat's milk and still enjoy a fantastic breakfast of mouth-watering homemade cereal.

Get Cheesy

If you are a geese lover like me, then you're lucky. This is another good option for using your goat's milk as you can make some delicious cheese with goat's milk. Not just about making cheese, you can make up to ten different kinds of cheeses that can be used in almost any recipe that includes cheese.

Make It Thicker

You can make delicious yogurt out of your goat's milk. If you have not attempted homemade yogurt before, you may need to make use of a yogurt maker to make the process a bit straightforward. Nevertheless, you can also make use of your crock-pot if you like. Irrespective of the method you opt for, just be aware that both yogurt and kefir can be made from your goat's milk.

6. Make Cajeta

You can make a delicious Mexican caramel sauce called Cajeta with goat's milk. So, make good use of your goat's milk; make this tasty sauce and spread it over mouth-watering homemade dessert.

Make Some Beautiful Soap

Soap making is one of the common and ways to use our goat's milk. So, if you are not aware, goat's milk creates some of the best homemade soap.

Other things you can do with your goat's milk include milkshake, pudding, caramel candy, ice cream, cottage cheese, cream cheese, buttermilk, goat cheese Soufflé, luscious lotion, and more.

Additional Tips and Warnings

- Be cautious of dogs in the neighborhood running loose. If a dog or coyote attacks your goats, make sure you check the neck for any hidden injury. Don't just assume the goat only has a broken leg.

- As mentioned earlier, goats can be aggressive, so you must act boldly around them, even if you do not feel like it.

- You are advised not to opt for a horned goat as a first-timer. You need to understand how to deal with them; otherwise, you could easily get hurt.

- As goats are raised for meat, dairy, or as pet, it's not ideal to name an animal you're raising for meat.

- Goats are very smart; they are capable of opening the latch on your fence. Get ready to change your fencing as required once you are familiar with the specific abilities of your herd.

- Kid goats taken away from their mother need extra attention from you. You will want to spend at least two hours daily with your goat. Surely, they will call you when they need attention.

- Goats love grass, weeds, trees, and bushes.
  Ensure that any tree you don't want to be
  destroyed isn't within their reach. When a
  standard size goat stands on its hind legs, it has
  a reach of 10 feet. So, any lower branches of
  tree in their vicinity are gone as they will prune
  them off before you realize.

- If keeping goats for meat, learn the consumers'
  preferences in your neighborhood. Muslims
  and Latinos can be great markets.

- It is essential to de-worm your goat. You will
  want to arrange an appointment with a
  veterinarian to work out a de-worming
  program. You can typically carry out the de-
  worming at home, but you will need expert

advice on the best timing to de-worm, depending on the season and your region.

- It is advisable to breed a doe (female goat) once a year. Some does can have babies two times in 18 months. Generally, goats reach the peak of their efficiency at 5 to 7 years old. In exceptional cases they continue to be serviceable even up to twelve years or fourteen years in rare cases.